AF488786
Jason Wh
Sickness

JASON WHITE

lives in Barrie, Ontario, Canada doing what he loves most: creating, and being a father. Jason is the father of five and grandfather of four. Jason enjoys volunteering in many capacities, and writing or creating in his wood shop or kitchen. Whatever he is doing, he likes to do it with his family.

Other Books Available
On Amazon

Passion
She
About Face
Reaching
Journey Home
Sleep: Evergreen Edition – Seasons Collection
Ransom Notes: A Macabre Hypothesis
Reflections: not so subtle words
Resurrect: So Below Edition – Seasons Collection
Healing
Reality
An Angrier Man
The Diary of a Warrior
LOVElier Days
The Way Aliens Take Over
The Patreon Files: Volume 1
Things I May Say – From Time-to-Time
The Fools Journey
Beautiful Disaster
Fucking Our Way to Freedom
Shattered
Monsters In My Closet
A Crazier Man
My Public Downfall

Sickness

Jason White

Damn,

that party was off the hook

I drank so much

and there were so many drugs too.

I am blessed to have friends like you.

What happened anyway?

Yo, I think I hooked up with that chick from the bar.

Where did we end up?

Shit, I barely remember a damned thing.

I need to brush my teeth

and drink an entire lake.

That stale pizza tastes as good as it could.

Shit, I spent all my rent money,

anybody got 20 bucks for smokes?

Can you spot me a quarter until payday?

I am still drunk,

I think I am going to puke.

Yo dude,

make sure your wife don't tell mine the truth,

she isn't cool like her.

I told her I'd be quick,

it's been two days, shit.

Give me another bump.

Can I fuck you lady again?

She's got the sweetest pussy.

Okay, I really gotta go.

I'll be in the doghouse for sure.

If she wants to bitch too much

I'll be back for more.

Sometimes I sit in my car
trying to compose myself
before I go into work.
It's funny too
that I am not the only one.
But we're supposed to be better,
what a joke.
More money, more problems,
that's for damned sure.
I take a few more pill,
polish off the bottle under my seat
and quickly tuck it back away.
Fuck,
how did I let it get to this point?
I'm on the brink of divorce
and I don't know my kids.
I spend more money on drugs
than I do on food.
The women, the affairs,
I am such a coward.
Constantly drowning my sorrows
and constantly creating more.
I wonder how much longer
I have to do this for.

I get home from another night out

and she's at the kitchen table crying.

I feel like shit,

for a moment.

But then that moment passes

and my ego takes over.

How the fuck can she be so selfish?

I work hard for this family,

I deserve to have fun once in a while.

She's angry, and sad, and confused.

She's hurt, and fragile, and exhausted.

Despite that she comes to hug me,

the look on her face is lightened just a little

now that she knows I am alright.

She gets a little closer,

her tears quit falling

and she drops her head.

She can smell another woman,

she falls silent and goes to bed.

Why do I do this shit?

I said I'd never be like my daddy

yet here I am.

I think she's going to leave me.

Maybe I should do something to make her stay.

It's Sunday

and I am sitting in church with my family.

It's been so long since I've been,

I wonder how many excuses she's made for me.

I look over at her,

damned she's so beautiful.

The happiness on her face is so radiant,

she's been waiting for me for so long.

She's been waiting for the man she knew.

I'm still here

buried so damned deep.

I wonder what my bros are doing.

I wonder what my side dish is doing.

I wonder if she's craving this cock.

Fuck,

it's only been three days since I made my hollow promise.

She can tell that I am not really here.

She can tell that I am pulling away.

This reality is too much for me.

I crawl back into bed.

A week in,

she's just checked the bank

and she's mad at me again.

To be honest,

I don't know how we will pay the rent.

Not because we couldn't

but because I can't keep the promise I made

I can't stand this,

I'll be back later.

Work is calling,

wondering where I've been.

She's calling too.

I don't know how she keeps hanging on.

I've fallen victim to these addictions.

She's a victim too,

they all are.

Goddamn I've missed this

the rush of the drugs

coursing my veins.

The freeing euphoria

of the alcohol.

My side piece

or some other juicy chick

keeping me warm for the night.

If this is so wrong

why does it feel so right?

I can't say I am surprised.

I came home and they were gone.

If I said I don't deserve this

I'd be wrong,

I'd be lying.

Lying, I am a liar.

I've made a game of it.

Not hiding my addictions;

pussy, drugs, alcohol.

No, it was considerably worse.

The promises to do better,

to meet her commitment to me.

Looks like I've lost this game.

I can't be alone,

so pitiful,

it didn't take too long.

I woke up the next morning

and picked up my phone,

called up my side piece and said

I guess you're my main bitch now.

I'll be right over, she said.

That night we partied harder than we had in a long time

I pretended to be happy,

I pretended to be free.

I let the clown out of his cage,

the part of me who hides the pain.

Pretending is my thing.

My reality is I can't deal.

Please come home, love.

I miss you.

I can't do this without you.

But you have been.

You've lived your own life for so long.

But I will change.

If you haven't changed yet

you won't if I come back home.

It's been six months.

What can I say?

She's right,

if I was going to change I would.

My side piece became my main bitch,

now she's gone too.

I guess she thought it would become me and her.

But you can't teach an old dog new tricks,

I guess.

At least I still have my friends.

And that one with the community wife.

I am so blessed to have friends like them.

Four months since I've seen my kids.

Fuck.

I am a goddamned asshole.

She's still protecting me,

telling the kids lies instead of the truth.

Why do I deserve this kindness?

Daddy has been really busy with work,

next time, my loves, next time.

Hi baby,

I know it has been a year.

Fuck,

I miss you and the kids.

I am going to rehab.

I want you back.

Let's see how you do.

I made it.

Thirty days seemed like a lifetime.

But I am clean.

I get to see my babies tonight.

Dinner was so damned awkward.

She's so suspicious of my commitment

and my kids don't even know me anymore.

I let the clown out of the cage,

they can't see me vulnerable.

How did I think I could do this?

I kiss them all good-bye

and I hit the nearest liquor store on the way.

She was right,

I will never change.

Three weeks later,

I've been back in the game since day one.

I'm hiding it better.

I need her,

she doesn't need me.

She wants me,

I don't want her.

It's a fucked up place to be.

I have to play the game smoother this time.

No more benders,

just quick shots of my addictions.

I've picked up fishing

I have it all in the bag,

this game is mine now.

I was the one calling the shots,

fooling her,

having my cake and eating it too.

But then,

one day I didn't come home.

My addictions got the better of me.

My sickness has been cured.